SECRETS OF PRODUCTIVE LIVING

(TIMELESS PRACTICAL LESSONS FROM THE ANT)

JOHN JAMES ABEKAH

JOHN JAMES ABEKAH

ISBN: 9798707964954
Imprint: Independently published

For further enquiries on the book or the author, please contact the address below:-

HE SENT HIS WORD PUBLICATIONS
P. O. BOX OS 2620 OSU
ACCRA- GHANA
TEL: 233 243 171 142

EMAIL: hshwpublications@gmail.com
You may check out the author's blog page:
http://jjabekahministries.com

JOHN JAMES ABEKAH

Table of Contents

JOHN JAMES ABEKAH

ACKNOWLEDGEMENT

I would say a very big thank you to the almighty God for giving me the greatest gift in life: the ability to become. And for also inspiring me to understand that there is no limit to what I can do and achieve in life.

"Our deepest fear is not that we are inadequate. Our deepest fear is that we are powerful beyond measure … As we let our light shine, we unconsciously give other people permission to do the same". Marianne Williamson

To all the people who have inspired me through their achievements and legacy of books, thank you so much.

JOHN JAMES ABEKAH

DEDICATION

I dedicate this book to my step-mother:
MADAM VICTORIA K. NEEQUAYE.
Thank you for making room in your heart for us and
sharing your life with us. As I look back to all these years, I
see you have been and continue to be an angel of the Lord
in our lives. May the Lord bless you with long life and good
health.

JOHN JAMES ABEKAH

PREFACE

King Solomon was the richest man to have ever lived. His net worth was estimated at $2.2 trillion during his lifetime. Apart from his unimaginable wealth, he also possessed something very rare but valuable: wisdom from God. By this wisdom, he became so sensitive to the happenings in the deep hearts of the people he had to deal with. When a man of such calibre speaks or writes anything, I believe his words should not be taken lightly. His observations about life and all its various facets are worthy of the deepest meditation.

King Solomon observed four very tiny insects upon the face of the earth which are exceedingly wise: ants, spider, locusts and rock badger. The observation of wisdom that these tiny insects bring to bear, reveal their instinctive applications of certain wisdom principles. Wisdom is the correct application of knowledge, fact or information to bring solutions to the problems that confront us. In this Series, I shall take various aspects of these insects to extract the wisdom nuggets they display for our consumption.

JOHN JAMES ABEKAH

INTRODUCTION

TEACHABILITY

Every human is born into this life with certain unique characteristics and features. What we become after we are born into this life, however, is determined largely by our environment and the human associations we keep. These two factors form the basis for what we hear and what we see. If we eventually become what we hear and see over a while, then our destiny is largely a product of the environment we function in.

Every human being comes into this life with at least one talent: obvious talents or hidden ones. Though abilities differ, a common gift we all possess is the ability to become. This I believe is the greatest gift anyone can ever have: the ability and willingness to become. This is what I term teachability.

The journey into becoming your future begins with the willingness to learn: look, see, hear and listen from your broad environment.

Pride, a strong obstacle to this ability and willingness to become, is not just the unwillingness to learn but the desire to learn from no other source but one's self only. To the proud person, no one knows anything they don't already know.

How willing and ready are you to learn from others? The fact that you are reading this little book is proof of your humility.

There is nothing worth knowing that God has not already placed within our reach. God, in His infinite wisdom, has sealed up all answers to the puzzles of our lives and destiny into other people and things around us. Your willingness to learn also from others will open up depth of answers to you.

WHY I WROTE THIS BOOK

"There be four things which are little upon the earth but they are exceeding wise:" Proverbs 30: 24

My purpose for putting this series together is to project to you each of these little creatures of wisdom with the intent of presenting the secrets of productive living. May this easy-to-read booklet be of maximum benefit to you. May the other three of this Little 4 Series bring an end to your quest for answers at this very stage of your life and particularly as you apply them to your life, may you make progress in your pursuits and be identified as a very fruitful and productive person in your field of play.

In this particular series: SECRETS OF PRODUCTIVE LIVING (TIMELESS PRACTICAL LESSONS FROM THE ANT), I'll be taking you on a very brief journey to show you that perfection is not synonymous to productivity. You don't have to be flawless or without fault to become what you will to become.

I have come to know by experience that our value in life is largely determined by how much value we are adding to the lives around us. How productive you are in your field will go a long way to open certain impossible doors of opportunities for you. Productivity has been defined by David O. Abioye as the products resulting from a set of activities. If you can have something tangible or intangible (like a service) to show for all the activities of your life, then you are productive. I visited the office of one great pastor in Ghana in the year 2010. The receptionist attended to me with some level of contempt until I brought out one of the products of my life bearing my name and picture. As if an eject bottom on her chair was pressed, she jerked up from her seat and stood, spoke to me more politely, made an instant phone call to the pastor's office and before I knew it, I was in the pastor's office being interviewed by his assistant.

Many are busy and full of activities and yet have no product to show for all their busy schedules. I want to help you to come out of an unproductive lifestyle. Remember that your value in life is greatly determined by the value you constantly add to the lives around you. A changed mindset can begin to do marvellous things. I wrote this book for you, read through it several times and put what you read into practice until it becomes your second nature and begins to have proofs in your life.

Go to the ant...consider her ways and
be wise" Proverbs 6:6

As little as the ant is, its ways are worth consideration.

The ants are a people not strong, yet it prepares....Proverbs 30:25

Have you ever wondered how ants have kept themselves from extinction while mightier species of animals are faced with possible total extinction? Even without taking the pain to describe an ant to you in this book, no human can convince me of his ignorance of what the insect ant looks like. They have made their presence relevant to every human home through the principles of productive living that we shall be considering in this book.

SOME INTERESTING FACTS ABOUT ANTS

1.   Like all insects, ants have six legs. Each leg has three joints. The legs of the ant are very strong so they can run very quickly. If a man could run as fast for his size as an ant can, he could run as fast as a racehorse.

2.   Ants can lift 20 times their body weight.

3.   An ant brain has about 250 000 brain cells. A human brain has 10,000 million so a colony of 40,000 ants has collectively the same size brain as a human.

4.   The average life expectancy of an ant is 45-60 days.

5. Ants use their antennae not only for touch but also for their sense of smell.

6. The head of the ant has a pair of large, strong jaws. The jaws open and shut sideways like a pair of scissors.

7. Adult ants cannot chew and swallow solid food. Instead, they swallow the juice which they squeeze from pieces of food. They throw away the dry part that is left over.

8. The ant has two eyes, each eye is made of many smaller eyes. They are called compound eyes.

9. The abdomen of the ant contains two stomachs. One stomach holds the food for itself and the second stomach is for food to be shared with other ants.

10. Like all insects, the outside of their body is covered with a hard armour this is called the exoskeleton.

11. Ants have four distinct growing stages, the egg, larva, pupa and the adult.

12. Biologists classify ants as a special group of wasps. (Hymenoptera Formicidae) There are over 10000 known species of ants.

13. Each ant colony has at least one or more queens. The job of the queen is to lay eggs which the worker ants look after.

14. Worker ants are sterile, they look for food, look after the young, and defend the nest from unwanted visitors. Ants are clean and tidy insects. Some worker ants are given the job of taking the rubbish from the nest and putting it outside in a special rubbish dump!

15. Each colony of ants has its smell. In this way, intruders can be recognized immediately.

16. Many ants such as the common Red species have a sting which they use to defend their nest.

17. The common Black Ants and Wood Ants have no sting, but they can squirt a spray of formic acid. Some birds put ants in their feathers because the ants squirt formic acid which gets rid of the parasites.

18. The Slave-Maker Ant (Polyergus Rufescens) raids the nests of other ants and steals their pupae. When these new

ants hatch, they work as slaves within the colony. The worker ants keep the eggs and larvae in different groups according to ages.

19.   At night the worker ants move the eggs and larvae deep into the nest to protect them from the cold. During the daytime, the worker ants move the eggs and larvae of the colony to the top of the nest so that they can be warmer.

20. If a worker ant has found a good source for food, it leaves a trail of scent so that the other ants in the colony can find the food.

21 Army Ants are nomadic and they are always moving. They carry their larvae and their eggs with them in a long column.

22.   The Army Ant (Ecitron Burchelli) of South America, can have as many as 700,000 members in its colony.

23. The Leaf Cutter Ants are farmers. They cut out pieces of leaves which they take back to their nests. They chew them into a pulp and a special fungus grows it.

24. Ants cannot digest leaves because they cannot digest cellulose.

(https://thebugsstophere.com/pest-control/interesting-facts-about-ants/)

CHAPTER ONE

BE TRUE TO YOURSELF

"But be doers of the word and not hearers only, deceiving yourselves"

James1:22

When you keep hearing instructions about life and you don't adopt them as a lifestyle then you are denying yourself of a better future. You were designed to live your life from the knowledge reserves you have accumulated over the years. Every 'new' knowledge or information that comes to you, especially the information that is instructional can bring you new and better experience provided you understand that piece of information so well and even more importantly act upon that instructional knowledge. On the other hand if all you do is to amass 'new' knowledge without a proportional application of it, you'll become very frustrated eventually. Act upon what you know for that is the ultimate purpose of knowledge. Action guided by knowledge is what will bring to you your desired change. If you are not doing what you know, why? The Bible describes that behaviour of constant pursuit of knowledge without doing what one knows as self-deception.

Refusing to tell yourself the truth is the greatest tragedy that can ever happen to you, self-deception. It is somewhat permissible to tell a lie or to be lied to by another but believing in your lies is unacceptable.

It is one thing to be faithful and a different thing to be sincere. Faithfulness is being true and genuine to others but sincerity is being true to yourself.

Why will someone lie to himself? I guess, sometimes, the truth is too hard, perhaps too bitter to accept. Until we accept the truth about ourselves, we are not ready for the profitable changes that can happen to us. Sincerity will not bow to flatteries when one knows that what others are saying about you is not true. Self-judgment or self-scrutiny is the starting place for sincerity. You don't have to be self-condemning in approach as you seek to be frank with yourself. It is very easy to be frank, blunt and straight forward when dealing with other people. Some can even go as far as being cruel when dealing 'truthfully' with others. Such people, I have found out, are mostly hypocrites. If each one can have 50% of the courage we use in telling other people the 'truth' to their face, in telling ourselves the truth, the world will become a better place. There can be no self-improvement until we become sincere with ourselves. Instead of being hard on others, be very hard on yourself and lenient towards others. You should stop demanding mountainous feats from others when you have not even required a pebble-like action from your self.

When you have told yourself the whole truth about yourself, then no criticism from a critique will be critical enough to sound like an insult or intimidating to your ears.

Find yourself, know yourself and be yourself.

If there is one single thing God would have you learn from the ant, it is this: "BEING TRUE TO YOURSELF",
"TELLING YOURSELF THE TRUTH",
"BEING SINCERE".

"The ants are a people not strong".

How many people will accept such comments about themselves from others without feeling insulted?

Do you have any form of deformity? Any inadequacies? If there are, you don't need to hide them or deny their existence. Accepting these facts about your personality does not mean you are exempted from a life of success, rather, it positions you at an advantage over those without them. Humans have a way of celebrating people who succeed despite their challenges than 'whole' people. It is more inspirational to hear and see success from people who overcame insurmountable and impossible obstacles than those who had an easy way out to success. Helen Keller said that blind minds are worse than blind eyes. I believe that for every lack in our lives, there are corresponding desires to succeed despite our 'deformities'. Your deformity is not an inability as long as you have the ability of self-improvement.

INSPIRATIONAL PEOPLE WITH DISABILITIES

HELEN KELLER

An American author, political activist and lecturer who is on the Alabama state quarter, Helen Keller was the first deaf and blind person to earn a college degree. Her story was famously portrayed in the play and film, The Miracle Worker, which documented how her teacher Anne Sullivan was finally able to develop a language that Helen could understand.

QUOTES FROM HELEN KELLER

'Optimism is the faith that leads to achievement. Nothing can be done without hope and confidence'.

'When one door of happiness closes, another opens; but often we look so long at the closed door that we do not see the one which has been opened for us'.

JOHN JAMES ABEKAH

*'The only thing worse than being blind
is having sight but no vision'.*

Helen wrote a total of 12 published books, including her spiritual autobiography, My Religion, and was also a member of the Socialist Party in America, and campaigned heavily for women's rights and other labour rights.

FDR

A beloved U.S. president who helped guide the nation successfully through World War II, President Franklin Delano Roosevelt is considered a great president and the entire time he was in office, FDR was also a wheelchair-user. Upon starting his political career in gusto, he contracted polio while drinking water at a campground and became paralyzed from the waist down.

QUOTES FROM FRANKLIN D. ROOSEVELT

"The only thing we have to fear is fear itself."

"When you come to the end of your rope, tie a knot and hang on."

"A smooth sea never made a skilled sailor."

Even though it wasn't made public until years later that he couldn't walk for fear of the public doubting his competency, FDR proved paralysis wasn't a roadblock to being a great leader.

STEVIE WONDER

One of the most beloved singers alive today, Stevie Wonder is a musician, singer and songwriter who was born blind. He was born six weeks early. The blood vessels at the back of his eyes had not yet reached the front and aborted their growth, hence his blindness.

QUOTES FROM STEVIE WONDER

'We all have ability. The difference is how we use it'.

'Just because a man lacks the use of his eyes doesn't mean he lacks vision'.

'The Lord that I serve says the impossible is unacceptable'.

Considered a child prodigy, Stevie signed with his first record label at age 11, Motown's Tamla label, and he's been performing since. Over his wildly successful music career, Stevie has recorded more than 30 U.S. top ten hits, including his singles

"Superstition," "Sir Duke" and "I Just Called to Say I Love You."

NICK VUJICIC

Nick Vujicic is another world-famous celebrity with a disability, and founder of Life Without Limbs - an organization for people with physical disabilities.

Vujicic was born in 1982 with no limbs. He claims that as a child he suffered ridicule and discrimination, and tried to commit suicide but, with time, he learned to see his potential.

QUOTES FROM NICK VUJICIC

*'Fear is the biggest disability of all.
And will paralyze you more than being
in a wheelchair'.*

'I was never crippled until I lost hope'.

*'You should never live according to
what you lack'.*

He is currently giving motivational talks around the world, has written several books and is a regular guest on talk shows and TV programs. He became very famous when starring in the touching short film "The Butterfly Circus".

SECRETS OF PRODUCTIVE LIVING

The ant is not a physically strong insect but more importantly, it does not comfort itself with a lie that strength is useless after all. It will be completely preposterous for the ant to say that strength is not important because it lacks it. That will be a negative way of trying to deal with a deficiency. Though physical strength may not be a necessary asset for the survival of the ant, it does not mean that strength is useless. Strength is necessary for those who possess it.

If you have not given birth yet, don't say children are not important. I know you may find some solace in saying that, but is that sincerity? Be truthful to yourself and then make arrangements to adopt one if you can't bear one by yourself.

When you accept yourself the way you are, you will begin to see your peculiarities and uniqueness from others.

Can I tell you something? You are special. Your uniqueness and power are in your difference from others. Why do you want to be like others when others what to be like you?

What makes the ant so special that even humans are instructed to go to the ant to learn? Do you realize that it is the "weakness" of the ant that makes it famous and not its "strength"?

It is the way you handle your "weakness" that makes you a reference point. Come on, arise, stop covering up, face your fears and confront your challenges. You are more than you can see with your eyes.

Listen with your heart, embrace the truth and get to work.

JOHN JAMES ABEKAH

CHAPTER TWO

THE PRINCIPLE OF
PREPARATION

Principles are the fundamental and universal laws that govern and guarantee the proportional outcomes of every cause of action. Principles will always work everywhere in the same way for everybody who cares to put them to work.

When a child of about seven years picks a viable orange seed and plants it in a conducive environment, the outcome of those actions will not be different from that of an eighty-seven-year-old professional farmer who does the same thing. If anything changes in the outcome, it will be as a result of a change in one of the variables.

Anytime you gain great and positive results in any area of your life, it's because you are doing something right even though you might not be consciously aware of the exact action. Similarly, if your relationship is failing, it's because you are doing the wrong things unconsciously. It is even possible you might be doing the right things wrongly.

When an unfriendly person decides to follow all the principle governing making more friends, one of which is being friendly, will end up with more friends than a naturally friendly person who decides to go against all the laws governing friendship which he has known and practised over the years.

On one of my birthdays, one of my good friends took me out shopping. I watched in amazement how he interacted freely with several different strangers and succeeded in some level of friendship with them. Later on, on my own, I began doing all the things I saw him do to get numerous friends. I was surprised at the number of friends, at least acquaintances I was getting at such a higher rate. I became uncomfortable with my sudden success because I felt I wasn't being real and secondly, I didn't think I could keep all those new friends.

But here is the point, what we may refer to as a person's personality includes a set of principles that have been practised over a long period until it becomes an unconscious part of the person. When we analyze the personality of a successful person, we derive the principles of success and when we synthesize the principles of success, we arrive at a successful personality.

In analyzing the nature of the ant, despite its lack of strength, we see a great fundamental and universal law instinctively at work in it thereby making it one of the little but very wise insects: the principle of PREPARATION.

Preparation is the process of making yourself ready for your immediate or distant future. In preparing, we go through a process to get ready for both the events that make you happy and those that will make you sad. We must prepare for both the adversities and opportunities in life. Only prior preparation can stabilize you in the moments of trouble. A prepared person will see all forms of opportunities in difficult moments when they come. An unprepared person on the contrary won't see opportunities even when they throw themselves at him. Since preparation for tomorrow is a requirement for great accomplishment, we must embrace the challenge and get skilful at preparing.

For one to become skilful at this all essential life skill: PREPARATION, one must look beyond the present and see far ahead. It entails mentally projecting the possible opportunities that will present themselves at every turn of event and getting ready for them. Preparation has a way of forcing out the details of life and empowering you to have control over life's surprises. Preparation will cut out waste of time and the waste of other equally important resources in your life.

WHY PEOPLE FAIL TO PREPARE

1.   People   can't   see   beyond   the   present circumstances.

People fail to prepare when it becomes a challenge for them to anticipate any major shift or change in their future from what it is now. 'Life has always remained this way and it shall forever remain so', is the silent anthem of those who will take preparation for granted.

2.   What happens to others cannot happen to them.

Deep down in the recess of our mind and heart, the natural and unnatural calamities that befall people cannot befall us.

3.   They are busy.

To be busy is a requirement for productivity in life. But it becomes counterproductive when we get too busy in the non-essentials of life. There have been times I got too busy as an attempt and a cover-up to avoid what was rather important and urgent.

4.   They don't have time.

There has never been enough time to accomplish everything you desire. And there will never be. 'I don't have time' is a myth. No one has time except we make time for the things we deem necessary and urgent. Every single day is a package of not less or more than 24 hours. This 24-hour package is renewed for each one daily and expires at the end of each day. No one has yet been able to store some two hours of Monday's and transferred it over to Tuesday to have 26 hours. From birth till death you'll always have 24 hours into your daily account. What you put into your hours every day will determine what your hours will put back into your life. Each of us will make time for what we deem necessary and important to us.

5. Procrastination

To anyone who will not prepare, there always seem to be a more ideal and better time to carry out what is necessary. It is a high attribute of every procrastinator. There is no better time to start preparing for tomorrow than right now. Yesterday would have been more appropriate. I was told a story of a group of five boys who agreed to plant some coconuts in their earlier days. The fifth boy refused to plant because he could not see when the coconut will germinate, grow up to bear fruits for them to enjoy. He felt the waiting will never end and he might be dead before the harvest time. Considering all these, he teased and even tried to discourage the others that planting coconut was not a great idea. The group left him alone and went ahead to plant their seeds. Of course, it was hard word both to plant and to wait for the harvest but it finally came. When the harvest came, this fifth boy recounted his regret and sang the most popular 'had I known is always at last' song. When you don't prepare, then you would have to learn how to sing this 'had I known is always at last' song.

6. It is too late

When you think it is already too late, you will not prepare. Convince yourself however, that it is better late than never. You see, the fifth boy after realizing his mistake, still felt it was too late to start all over again. At every point or stage in your live, you can always initiate the beginning of a new cycle that can create for you a better experience. It's better to start late than not to start at all. When you are indeed motivated, it's never too late.

7.   What will happen is still going to happen anyway

This is yet another reason why some fail to prepare. You know, your preparation will not immune you against adversities and opportunities but preparation will put you in a better place to embrace them when they come.

PREPARING FOR ADVERSITY

As important as preparation for opportunities are to taking advantage of them for advancement, preparing against adversity is also absolutely necessary else they take advantage of you.

LOSS OF JOB

I know a man who lost his job under very unfavourable circumstances. Even though he did not die, his life came to an end. His health began to deteriorate and his beautiful family broke apart. All he did before was to work at a job. He never worked on himself, he never anticipated how a dedicated man like himself will be released off his post. Most people stop learning the moment they become gainfully employed. But the greatest job security anyone can ever possess is constant self-development. Don't stop learning, keep learning and outgrow your current position, make the job depend on you. When you have so prepared yourself for job loss, you will not even see it when it happens because then it will simply be a transition from a less venture to a more profitable venture. As you keep doing that, you will be so large in a capacity that you end up building chains of businesses for yourself.

INCAPACITATION

What will happen should you become incapacitated? When your legs won't function again as a footballer, lose sight as a driver, can't speak again as a preacher or a public speaker, what will you do? You see, these circumstances have befallen some people, but the greater devastation was as a result of the shock that accompanied these adversities. It is only after they can overcome the shock that they are ever able to undergo the process of recovery. Those who couldn't rise above the shock had to live with that predicament forever. When you are mentally prepared for this, it places you in a better position to manage it till recovery point. Losing life savings or capital can have similar effects. It is the preparations you have made by way of insurance, investments into knowledge, generosity towards family, friends and even strangers that will sustain you. Start preparing.

OLD AGE

Old age is as predictable as changes in life and yet many will not give it a thought until it is too late. The only painful way to escape death is an early death. Those who find old age as restful days are those who prepared for it. Whether you like it or not, when you mandatorily retire from active service at 60 or 65 or voluntarily at an earlier age, you may still have at least 20 more years to live. Have you given serious thought to your pension plans? But more important than your pension plans, your children. Invest greatly in their scholarly training. Also, invest spiritually and morally into them else even though they'll be successful, they'll have no compassion or respect for you when you are old or any other older person. I have known some fathers who abandoned their wives and children. Their life in old age was not palatable at all. I know few mothers also who by following all the pleasures of their youthful stages, gave little consideration to the plight of their children. They paid heavily for it in their old ages.

DEATH

Death, just like birth, is one thing that none of us can skip. Just as birth is the only entrance into this world, death is the only exit from this life. What are you going to do when a loved one dies? In his book, "When Sorrow Comes, Let Not Your Heart Be Troubled", Norman Vincent Peale elaborates on three key faulty perceptions about death can make the pain very unbearable: firstly, that death is a grim reaper, hooded and hostile, secondly, focusing on the lifeless body rather than the spirit that has been set eternally free from the body and thirdly that the departed one has lost more than has gained. In preparing for the departure of a loved one, be it a spouse, a child, a parent or a very close friend, we must remember that those departed people feel no pain at all and if they committed their lives to the Creator before their death, then it becomes even better in their departure.

The first-ever funeral I conducted was for a 14-year-old girl. It was indeed a sad event considering the crowd that gathered at the funeral. In the course of delivering a short sermon, I was inspired to recount all the painful challenges that other teenagers of her age usually endure and sometimes how miserable they end up when they are not properly guided. We concluded that it was more profitable then for our friend who had departed because she had escaped all those possible pains. That understanding instantly lightened up the crowd at the funeral grounds.

The ants are not strong with regards to storms so they prepare their food in summer.

Since no scientific invention has discovered a death cure yet, we must all prepare against death. As you prepare to handle the death of a loved one in a composed manner, you must equally prepare for your death. I don't mean preparing for funeral arrangement, even though that too is absolutely necessary, but life after death. I believe there is life after death. I believe in heaven and hell. I believe in eternal judgment and the lake of fire. I believe in the totality of the Bible.

> *"And as it is appointed unto men once to die, but after this the judgment".*
>
> *Hebrews 9:27*

After your death, you will stand before your Maker to give an account of your life on the earth. But more importantly, if you gave your life to Jesus Christ while on earth and lived according to His dictates, you will be ushered into eternity with Him. On the other hand, if you rejected Him and had nothing to do with Him while on earth then that will earn you eternity with the Devil in the Lake of fire.

A wise man has said: 'It is better to live your life as though heaven existed and die only to discover that it was not so, than to live your life as if there were no hell, only to die afterwards to realize that you had been deceived'. That will be the most terrible mistake any man would commit.

Read this true story from the bible for better insight

"Now there was a certain man of great wealth, who was dressed in fair clothing of purple and delicate linen and was shining and glad every day. And a certain poor man, named Lazarus, was stretched out at his door, full of wounds, desiring the broken bits of food which came from the table of the man of wealth; and even the dogs came and put their tongues on his wounds.

And in time the poor man came to his end, and angels took him to Abraham's breast. And the man of wealth came to his end and was put in the earth. And in hell, being in great pain, lifting his eyes he saw Abraham, far away, and Lazarus on his breast. And he cried and said, Father Abraham, have mercy on me and send Lazarus, so that he may put the end of his finger in water and put it on my tongue, for I am cruelly burning in this flame. But Abraham said, Keep in mind, my son, that when you were living, you had your good things, while Lazarus had evil things: but now, he is comforted and you are in pain. And besides, there is a deep division fixed between us and you, so that those who might go from here to you are not able to do so, and no one may come from you to us.

And he said, Father, I request that you will send him to my father's house; for I have five brothers; and let him give them an account of these things, so that they may not come to this place of pain. But Abraham said, They have Moses and the prophets; let them give ear to what they say. And he said, No, father Abraham, but if someone went to them from the dead, their hearts would be changed. And he said to him, If they will not give attention to Moses and the prophets, they will not be moved even if someone comes back from the dead". Luke 16:19-31

At the end of the story, this Rich man, more than anything else, wanted his brothers to know about life after death. Will you prepare today? It begins by inviting Jesus Christ into your life. Click this link to do that now: TURNING POINT.

PREPARING FOR OPPORTUNITIES

It is your preparation that determines the opportunities that come to you. Since opportunity is a favourable circumstance that offers you an advantage to go a step further in your pursuits, when you have not prepared, you won't see the opportunities when they even present themselves to you.

NEW/ BETTER EMPLOYMENT

In preparing for a better career opportunity, it was Jim Rohn who said, 'When you become better, everything becomes better, when you change, everything changes'. In preparing for better employment, you must become more valuable than you are present.

Employment and deployment might appear the same but their difference exists in their philosophy. If you will consider your current engagement as a place of deployment rather than employment, it will push you a little further in improving upon yourself maximally. At your place of employment, someone must place a demand on you to give out to receive a salary. But in deployment, you are self-motivated to give out your best. With the attitude of deployment you are willing to give off your best because your employer or competitors are no longer your reason for doing the things you do, rather you become the competitor of the vast potential left untapped within you.

Improve yourself. Enhance your life skills: communication skills, team player skills, people and marketing skills just to mention a few.

I read the story of a young man who has accomplished great feats in a very amazing way. He started as a pupil's teacher. Unknown to his colleague pupil teachers in the same school, he was undertaking a medical course via distance education. He looked very odd among his colleague teachers because he always had something doing. Some even accused him of being very unfriendly and anti-social because he will not join them in their very avoidable social activities during 'free' periods. He didn't have the luxury of leisure hours. It was before his day of graduation that they got to know as he gave them his breath seizing invitation card.

After that graduation, he never returned to the classroom as a pupil's teacher again. He began practising medicine and shortly after enrolled in the law school too. When you start preparing for a more productive life, opportunities will abound for you.

TRAVELS

Prepare for travels. Prepare for moving temporarily or permanently intermittently. In getting ready, there are a whole lot of things involved. Find out all you can about where you will be moving to. Know about the cost of living there, few governmental policies, demographics and even labour laws. You can't just move and go anywhere, which will make you a total stranger indeed. It's okay to find out about a few technical issues about where you are seeking to move to from the internet. But for practical, day-to-day issues, it will be more appropriate to get information from human beings who live there or have been there before.

REAL ESTATE

Physiological needs of humans are the lowest level of Maslow's hierarchy of needs. That makes it the most essential thing a person needs to survive. They include the need for shelter, water, food, warmth, rest, and health. At this level, a person's instinct to survive becomes the motivating force to pursue such needs.

Preparing therefore to have a place to lay your head should be embraced early. Whether building, buying or renting a building, you will need to make up your mind and then begin to prepare towards it. There are countless opportunities around you to get what you want when you are prepared.

MARRIAGE AND FAMILY

Stability is one of the products of preparation. If there is any human endeavour that needs stability than any other thing in this life, it is the marital and family life. Changing your home, job or friends have no daring consequences and abysmal if any at all. But the repercussion for changing a marriage partner, dare to say, is eternal. Those who have undergone that will do all they can to cover up and present a kind of 'everything is fine' portrait to the rest of the world. But the dent has eternal consequences.

A countless number of people rather prepare for a wedding ceremony (a less than 24 hours event) and never give the slimmest thought to preparing for the marital life itself (a lifetime commitment) which commences a day after the wedding event.

As important as preparation for the wedding ceremony, to make it a successful event is, don't do that at the expense of the marriage itself. Every preparation you put in for the wedding ceremony is all about other people but preparing for the marriage is about the marrying couple. Make yourself ready for the marriage life

Preparation involves planning. Planning is the process of putting together a set of practical steps of action to attain your desire. A plan takes into account who you are, what you have, where you are now and how to get to where you need to be. This explains why anyone who will not plan for the next phase of his life will have a hard time.

"It shows you the shortest route to your destination"

Mike Murdock

"The ants are a people not strong, yet they prepare ..."

Proverbs 30:25

Personalities And Principle

It is people that carry out activities to produce results. It's a fact that the facial beauty of a woman has nothing to do with the "deliciousness" of the food she cooks. It does not matter whether a man or a woman prepared a meal. If either applies the principles or the setup rules governing delicious meals, the meal prepared must respond appropriately.

It is people that carry out activities, but the principles they employ is what brings about the kind of results they get. Principles have no respect for your personality. So, whether the ants are strong or weak, their application of the principle of preparation should bring them the required results.

Even though the ants lack strength, they lock themselves up in leveraging principles. As necessary as a high academic IQ is to pass an exam, the one who does not possess it should not fail. Anyone who does not possess a high academic IQ does not require it to pass his exams. Both the one who has a high intelligent quotient and the one who does not possess such must both lock themselves up into the principle of preparation at various degrees to have successful outcomes.

One of the laws of preparation states that: 'Know what you are about, what it requires and then get serious with action steps to get it done'. The quality of your preparedness will determine your outcome.

The ant judges itself, tells itself the truth that it has no strength to withstand the impending change in season. The ants can prepare long ahead of time against the future. That is what keeps them from extinction.

Now, concerning death, none of us is strong, but that is not the most important thing. The most important issue is what you are going to do about the fact that you shall also die? How are you preparing to meet death? After your time here is over, your creator will bring you to judgment. Most people don't really like this aspect of the Bible but it is an unchangeable fact. Like the ant, each of us must prepare against the judgment day.

A time will come when you will raise a family and would have to care for your family and even others. It will surely happen. But are you preparing for it?

5 PREPARATION CAPSULES

"Failure to prepare is preparing to fail".

DR. MIKE MURDOCK

"It is better to prepare for a crisis than later try to cure it".

DR. MENSAH OTABIL

"The best defence is to be vigilant and prepared".

BISHOP N.A.TACHIE-YARBOI

"I will prepare and some day my chance will come".

ABRAHAM LINCOLN

"So Jotham became mighty because he prepared his ways before the LORD his God".

2Chronicles 27:6

"You don't need a century to effect a change you only need effective preparation to provoke unusual transformation".

DR. DAVID OYEDEPO

CHAPTER THREE

SENSITIVE TO TIME

"The ants are a people not strong, yet they prepare their food in the summer."

Proverbs 30:25

Some things are best done only at certain times. To everything, there is a time.

I n his book, "SECRETS OF THE RICHEST MAN WHO EVER LIVED", Dr Mike Murdock explained that time is the most important gift God gave you. It behoves you then to trade it for any other thing you desire in your life. Whatever you don't have in your life is what you have been unwilling to trade your time for.

Time is a very necessary part of the equation of success.

When we come to the understanding that every time and season has a peculiar product it produces, then we will stop pressing undue labour to produce what that time is not meant to produce. I have shared more insight on this in my book SEASONAL DYNAMICS. You may want to check it out.

Naturally, the sun does not shine during the winter season, neither does the rain pour down in the dry season. Instead of forcing to produce things in their off-seasons, let's begin to discern what each season is set to bring and align our lives with it.

Why do ants gather their food in the summer? Though there are various seasons throughout the year, we generally know of two that stand out: sunny and rainy season in this part of our world. In other parts of the world, there is the spring, autumn, summer and winter. The Bible, however, refers to two of the form of summer and winter.

Winter is the season of rain when the temperature falls to the freezing - point. People with no means of heating their houses suffer because of the cold. Travelling especially on the waters becomes a real challenge.

The ant without strength has no chance of survival in times like this.

Summer on the other hand is very hot and without rain. It is a time of harvest and a lot of activities.

"He that gathereth in the summer is a wise son".

Proverbs 10:5

Back to why ants gather in summer.

Summer is the proper time for harvest. The wisdom of the ant is in knowing the proper thing to do at its proper time. Doing the right thing at the wrong time makes the action wrong.

Some things don't just work right at certain times of our lives.

I have also realized that adversities are a normal part of human lives. Each one of us should therefore prepare against that day of adversity because few people will respond well to words of encouragement at such times. In times of trouble, what you have already stocked on your inside is what will well up strongly in you for encouragement and sustenance.

"If thou faint in the day of adversity, thy strength is small".

Proverbs 24:10

"A wise man is strong, yea, a man of knowledge increaseth strength".

Proverbs 24:5

The strength of the wise is not in the use of his muscle but applied knowledge. When you fail in times of adversity then your knowledge base is either inadequate or inaccurate.

The ant gathers what it will need at the appropriate time. This is the time to gather adequate information about marriage and family before you enter into it. Then when the marriage crises arise you will not be broken on any occasion.

SENSITIVITY

"And the children of Issachar, which were men that had an understanding of the times, to know what Israel ought to do".

1 Chronicle 12:32

Sensitivity is an ability to respond to environmental changes or movements through the senses. It is also the proneness to respond to opportunities and timeliness of certain actions. Sensitivity is discernment, perception and understanding of the times.

One of the nuggets of wisdom the ant has is this sensitivity, natural instinctiveness, somehow they just know the season has changed.

One key to becoming sensitive is to be closer to the most sensitive person in the universe; God the Holy Spirit. When you are consistently closer to him, he activates this nature of his that is already in you.

Sensitivity to time is wisdom.

CHAPTER FOUR

TAKING ACTION

"Go to the ant you, thou sluggard,
consider her ways and be wise".

Proverbs 6:6

If there is anything in this world that changes visions or ideas into reality, it is taking the appropriate massive actions. People who seem to be rising consistently in life are people who take a lot of actions. As important as consulting with a medical doctor is, it is following his prescription that will change your health condition. Knowledge about a condition and a better understanding of the whole circumstance is crucial when it comes to overturning any undesirable situation. But you will agree with me that these two: knowledge and understanding only put you in a better position to do something about the situation. Yes, they empower you for action. If after you have been empowered you still do not take action, then the situation will persist. Only appropriate action can get things done. Stop putting off the things you must do and get to the action. Doing what you know is as important as knowing what to do to turn things around.

The ants take many little steps every day. Your goal is big, your vision might be very large but it will take plenty of little steps every day to get you closer to its achievement. Don't be overwhelmed by the size of the task ahead of you, simply take several little steps daily, for, after all, that is the way things were design to work: little, little things make up the big things of life.

This very lesson or principle is what this little insect embodies for our scrutiny. The diligence of the ant is a course or programme for anyone who desires unlimited productive life to undertake.

As I write this chapter, I'm gazing at an endless parade of red ants. They are "tidying up" the mess of what looks like bread crumbs left on the ground and it's only in the early hours of the morning. Anytime you "undisciplinely" eat and refuse to tidy up the crumbs from the ground, you have called for a parade. They will come unfailingly. Their diligence, to me, is uncompromising, very committed to their call to duty. To an ant, it can never gather enough. As long as rain has not dropped to the ground, it's an opportunity for them to gather.

According to Jesus' definition of wisdom, it is knowledge with action, acting out what we know.

KNOWLEDGE + ACTION = WISDOM

"Therefore whosoever heareth these sayings of mine and doeth them I will liken him to a wise man, which built his house upon a rock."

Matthew 7:24

"But be doers of the word and not hearers only, deceiving your selves".

James 1:22

If after you have done all the research and wide consultations and still don't do what must be done but still expect things to be different, then you are deceiving yourself. Why should you invest heavily financially and still refuse to carry out the recommendations received from the professionals?

ACTION - KNOWLEDGE = FOOLISHNESS

SECRETS OF PRODUCTIVE LIVING

"The labour of the foolish wearieth
every one of them, because he
knoweth not how to go to the city"

Ecclesiastes 10:15

Taking any action that has no knowledge basis will be inappropriate. When we do things without consulting the past or reference to history then we will constantly be repeating the past mistakes and that will get us nowhere in life. If you are seeking to accomplish a feat that others have already and severally carried out successfully, and you overlook their accomplishments, by not seeking from them their secrets, through their available materials that will be described as foolishness.

So from these three equations above, we see that labour or action is an essential part of the equation of wisdom and productivity. The ants work hard. You too should make diligence a part of your life. You can't have your dreams fulfilled without your input. Hard work is the only cure for a hard life.

Once a while we drop food over the heads of ants as we do to our pets. Ants won't come and sit around your table when they smell you are about to have lunch or dinner, they are used to searching out for their opportunities. If we are to be as wise as ants, then after not finding the opportunities we are seeking, we should move on to create those opportunities for ourselves and even others. I know people who have been refused employment because they were "over qualified". If no one wants to employ you, then deploy yourself.

You have a potential vision and dream, rise and begin to take the appropriate steps to bring it into reality. Procrastination is an unconscious denial of the birth of another great product or essential service associated with your name, shake it off.

UNUTILISED OPPORTUNITY

I saw a beautiful and yet heart-throbbing picture in the Songs of Solomon of the Holy Bible about the consequences of not utilizing the opportunities that come our way.

I was asleep, but my heart waked: It is the voice of my beloved that knocketh, saying, Open to me, my sister, my love, my dove, my undefiled; For my head is filled with dew, My locks with the drops of the night. I have put off my garment; how shall I put it on? I have washed my feet; how shall I defile them? My beloved put in his hand by the hole of the door, And my heart was moved for him. I rose to open to my beloved; And my hands droppeth with myrrh, And my fingers with liquid myrrh, Upon the handles of the bolt. I opened to my beloved, But my beloved had withdrawn himself and was gone. My soul had failed me when he spake: I sought him, but I could not find him; I called him, but he gave me no answer. The watchmen that go about the city found me, They smote me, they wounded me; The keepers of the walls took away my mantle from me.

Songs of Solomon 5:2-7

This scenario is about a lady and her lover. This lady was in a sleepy state when she heard a knock on her door. That sleepy state is the perfect point that solutions seek to attach themselves to us. In that state, she was in-between sleep and wake.

That sleepy state is best reached through meditation or practising quietness of mind. In that state, an idea easily dawns on you like a light bulb.

An idea, according to the MacMillan Dictionary is "A thought that you have about how to do something or how to deal with something". So an idea could be the solution to a problem that we have been seeking, an innovation or an invention. An idea, more importantly, is an opportunity-seeking to gain entrance into our world. It holds the key to a whole new world of doing things.

Unfortunately, this lady began to outline excuses just like each one of us does. Due to the unusual, unpredictable and unbelievable nature of the ideas that come to us at first sight, the immediate natural reaction to that idea is: 'This is impossible '. "This has never been done". "This idea might require too much capital which I don't have". 'I don't think I qualify to accomplish this task".

Unfortunately, many great visions through the finding and giving of excuses are denied access into our world. But just imagine this world without electricity, and yet the discovery of this great and profitable energy began as an idea in the head of an individual. What will happen to our world if you keep sending your ideas to Mr. Excuse? Don't you think the idea that flashed through your mind yesterday is a possibility? And that it can become real through your efforts?

After we have given excuses, sometimes, these ideas try to force themselves on us. Sometimes you go to places and you see strangers try to talk about 'your' idea or even trying to implement what you are still wrestling within a way that makes you feel jealous. You better get to work now!

TIMELY RESPONSE
Some opportunities need to be embraced within a set time. The wisdom, favour and strength that is needed to carry out certain assignments come along with the vision and idea. When your response is timely, all these are at your disposal. On the other hand, when you decide to put them off till a 'better' time, you would have to generate your energy to accomplish it when you now think you are ready.

As an author, I have written three chapters of a book straight at one sitting. It is so sweet and sweatless. This happens when I respond quickly to an idea, inspiration or "revelation". I have also equally sat for hours with a blank page on several occasions, no stroke of ink scratched the surface of my plain white sheet. I could hardly come up with any line of sentence. This has always been the result after I have put off an idea, inspiration or revelation for writing until a "more appropriate" time.

Ideas withdraw themselves when not responded to. Opportunities move into oblivion when refused an opening. The opportunity withdraws itself from a man who is not ready to work it out and seeks a ready and willing person.

RIGHT ACTION, WRONG TIMING

This lady finally decided to respond and do something with this idea. She rose and chased the good man. She went out to do the right thing at the wrong time, just like an ant who comes out to gather food during the rainy or winter season. There is nothing wrong in hard work but there is everything wrong with it doing it at the wrong time.

She was found by the watchmen of the city who usually carried out their duties at odd hours to ensure the security of others. They saw the presence of this "good' woman at such a time as a threat to their objective.

I can recollect about twelve years ago, an old man of about seventy years came to my school with a heavy load on his head. He had very simple but interesting novels he had written, published and wanted to sell to our students. With all the energy he had, he spoke and moved very slowly in presenting his storybooks to my grade five kids. Some of the smart kids tried very hard to hold back laughter as they watched with shock the patience of this old man in examining and counting every single coin he received from them. I forgot to assist this man as I was completely carried away by the numerous questions running through my mind about the old man: why now? What had he been doing? Has he got kids? Where are they? Why are they not helping him? Is my life also going to be like this old man? How much will he even be able to make from these books considering the pace at which he is moving? And blah blah blah. I didn't want to be judgmental toward him but rather toward myself.

The security personnel that should have protected her rather beat her up, bruised her and took away her covering and all source of comfort. Why? They became suspicious of her actions and intentions. When you over delay in carrying out your ideas, people become very suspicious of your actions and intentions when dealing with you and could make them adopt a more careful posture towards you. Get up and start pursuing the fulfilment of the ideas, visions and dreams that are buried in your heart now.

As wise as the ant is, it is not able to stand certain environmental changes. It knows it and avoids it completely by gathering its required needs at the right time.

"Now that it is the day, I must do the work of he who sent me for there comes a time where no man can do any work"

John 9:4

Jesus recognizes that there is an appropriate time for labour. There comes a time when the watchmen on the wall would come out to make their rounds in the city. May you never meet these watchmen as they make their rounds in the city. Rise and accept responsibility now.

CONCLUSION

Whatever you don't have today and can't have in your future is not a requirement for you to be fulfilled in life. Productivity in life isn't about what you don't have but what you do with what you have. That is wisdom. Despising what you have and focusing on what others have that you lack is not wisdom.

When David confronted Goliath DeGiant, he had no breastplate, helmet, shield, sword or javelin but had something else, a sling or catapult with stones. Do you know that with what he had in his hands he brought down the giant? The day you would realize that what you have was given to you by God and that it is as anointed and blessed as what you are looking at in the hands of you friends, then mountains will be levelled before you.

As far as your life is concerned, there are several things you can change, if you don't, you'll be held responsible. However, some things are just beyond your ability to changing them, the only thing you can do is to learn to live with them; endure them. I believe that realizing these things will help you to stay free from anxiety.

Mr. Zacchaeus was a rich man but was a very short man who needed to see Jesus Christ. His height was a disadvantage to him because a crowd always followed Jesus Christ everywhere. Because he was a sincere man, he did not pretend about what he didn't have, he faced it and sought for an alternative way out. He looked for a tree taller than himself and climbed on it. He saw Jesus. That is wisdom.

Do you think you are handicapped? There is no human being living who wasn't handicapped at some point in their lives. Your 'handicapness' will become your disability when you don't self-improve yourself. Self-improvement will push off every limitation forced on you by your handicaps. Rise, look beyond what you don't have and you would realize your most profitable and untapped endowment.

There is the story of Joni Eareckson Tada who as a teenager broke her neck when she drove into a shallow lake in1967. Ever since she was paralyzed from the neck down but the most amazing thing about Joni is that after two years of rehabilitation she has been just as active and as productive as any normal (non-disabled) person if not more. She is an internationally known painter (painting with a brush between her teeth), she has written over 48 books, recorded several musical albums and is actively involved as an advocate for disabled people. Not only is she the president and founder of an organization that accelerates Christian ministry in the disability community, but she is also a recipient of many national awards, including "Churchwoman of the year" in

1993 by the Religious Heritage Foundation, was named the 2011 Honorary Chairman of the National Day of Prayer. (Life Story Foundation/Joni And Friends)

POSTSCRIPT

Knowledge is the prize for any great future. Understanding is the anchor that keeps you hooked up to a consistent successful life. Wisdom is the principal thing. These are the keys this book has placed in your hands forever.

You were made in the image and likeness of God. The ant will no longer be wiser than you.

TURNING POINT

It continues to amaze me to know that our life is a collection of the decisions we have made. Each of us has the singular honour of deciding what our future should be like by the decision-making ability that God has given us.

I consider the wisest decision any one can make in this life is that one decision that affects his or her live eternally. Your life on earth as compared to your life in eternity is like the smoke of fire; it is soon gone. As you stand at the edge of time you can make that most important decision that forever changes your final dwelling place in eternity; life with Christ.

Every human being is a sinner and at a point in our life should come to Jesus Christ. He is the only Saviour of the human soul. Make that all-important decision today, come to Him. He will save you and give you a new beginning.
Pray with me aloud:

Father, I am sorry for walking in my sins all this while. I come to you because you gave me Jesus for my salvation. Thank you for loving me this much. Jesus, you took my place on the cross that I might have eternal life. I receive your gift of salvation and life eternal. Thank you for saving me, now I know I am born again and a part of your family. Amen.

Congratulations! If you have just prayed this prayer, you have received God's eternal gift of salvation, you are born again. Let me know of your decision to trust Christ by writing or emailing to the address below. I will be glad to have that privilege of helping you grow in this new life you have received.

HE SENT HIS WORD PUBLICATIONS
P. O. BOX OS 2620, OUS
ACCRA-GHANA.

E-MAIL: hshwpublications@gmail.com

ABOUT THE AUTHOR

JOHN JAMES ABEKAH is an ordained minister of the Gospel, an Inspirational Teacher, a Motivational Speaker, an Author, a Blogger and an Associate Pastor of Accra-based, Faith Miracle Church International.

He holds a Basic Certificate & Leadership Certificate from the Word of Faith Bible Institute (WOFBI) and a Diploma in Pastoral Ministries from the Victory Bible Training Institute (V.B.T.I.) respectively. He holds a Bachelor of Education in Basic Education (English) from the University of Cape Coast, Ghana.

J. J. Abekah has a mandate from God emphasizing on Knowledge of the Truth. This he continues to express through his teachings, talks, books and blogs resulting in total liberty for his listeners and readers. He has a burden to see people walk in divine knowledge, revelation, wisdom, and understanding.

J. J. Abekah is married to Mary Joyce and blessed with four children: Wise, Life, Favour, and Phebe. He resides in Accra, Ghana.

You may check out the author's blog page:
http://jjabekahministries.com

OTHER BOOKS BY THE AUTHOR

SEASONAL DYNAMICS: UNDERSTANDING YOUR SEASONS AND MAKING MAXIMUM USE OF YOUR EXPERIENCES

There are always various set periods between the commencement and completion of an assignment in life. It

is the unknown "gap" between your present and the future that makes it necessary for you to closely examine the various periods of your life to ensure that you do not do anything that would abort your dreams or cause a premature or pre-term delivery of your God-destined purpose.

In this book, you'll discover the most important keys in the various seasons of your life:

*Season of Rejection *Season of Disloyalty
*Season of Preparation *Season of Isolation
*Season of Unfair Treatment *Season of Learning
*Season of Delay *Waiting Season and many more …
You may check out more about this book:

• https://amzn.to/38WLUKV

BEWARE OF FOOLS (ESCAPING THE WEB OF WRONG ASSOCIATION)

The vicious cycle of wrong thoughts, wrong choices, wrong actions and wrong outcomes can be broken when you identify and break away from that one wrong person in your life.

In this yet another masterpiece, BEWARE OF FOOLS: ESCAPING THE WEB OF WRONG ASSOCIATION, the author John James Abekah unveils a host of wrong people around you and equips you to break off from them and from the fool in particular. You will:

*Discover that wrong association, indeed, is a slow poison

*Identify and connect with a true friend

*Undo the generational effects of wrong associations on your destiny

*And many more...

You may check out more about this book on this link: https://amzn.to/35SxUQD

ONE LAST THING...

Thank you for taking the time to read Secrets of Productive Living. If you enjoyed this book or found it useful, I'd be very grateful if you would post a short review on Amazon. Your support really does make a difference and I read all the reviews personally so I can get your feedback and make this book even better.

If you would like to leave a review then all you need to do is click the review link on this book's page on Amazon here:

Thanks again for your support.